BREAK OUT

LIVING YOUR OWN EMANCIPATION PROCLAMATION

NATHAN PATRICK

WWW.NATHANPATRICK.COM

For information about permission to reproduce selections from this book, write to: nathanpatrick111@gmail.com.

All Scripture quotations are taken from the New International Version unless otherwise noted.

The Holy Bible, New International Version, ©1973, 1978, 1984 by International Bible Society. Used by permission of International Bible Society.

Contemporary English Version, The Promise™ ©1995, Thomas Nelson, Inc. All rights reserved. Used by permission.

The Living Bible, ©1971 by Tyndale House Publishers, Wheaton, Illinois 60187. All rights reserved. Used by permission.

New Revised Standard Bible, ©1989, by the Division of Christian Education of the National Council of the Churches of Christ in the U.S.A. All rights reserved. Used by permission.

The New Testament in Modern English (Revised Edition), ©1958, 1960, 1972, J.B. Phillips. All rights reserved. Used by permission.

ISBN 978-0-9850395-0-9 (pbk)

ISBN 978-0-9850395-1-6 (ebook)

Table of Contents

Introduction
1

Chapter 1
Freedom, Anyone?
5

Chapter 2
Prison Break
17

Chapter 3
Wrecking Ball
32

Chapter 4
No More Building
43

Chapter 5
Just Say 'No'
53

Chapter 6
Flying Fearlessly
65

Chapter 7
Free To Be
75

Chapter 8
Freedom For All
83

Chapter 9
Dreams 'R' Us
93

Chapter 10
What The World Needs Now
104

Chapter 11
Living And Giving Freedom
113

Chapter 12
Moving On
122

INTRODUCTION

Freedom is on everyone's mind. Personal freedom is not limited to time or place. It is only limited by our ability to recognize our right to have it and to reclaim it after we have given it away.

This book comes from a series of lessons that I taught to my spiritual community. The ten points that you will encounter in this book came from a list of practical steps I taught at the end of one of my lessons. They were so well received that I printed copies for everyone and distributed them at our next session. The response continued to be so positive that eventually I wrote an entire series of lessons based upon this action list. This book is a result of teaching and sharing these lessons with others and the need for this information to be disseminated into a greater dimension.

I use Bible quotations along with other sources in my teachings. All writers are encouraged to "write what they know." My life and teachings have been based on the

Christian teachings but they have in no way stilted or hampered my journey. My philosophy that I live by and encourage my fellow travelers to live by is this: "Take what you can use and throw away the rest." Please do not feel that the Bible quotations are given in a spirit of "law and gospel," but I do feel that there is much wisdom in these scriptures just as there is much wisdom from other sources I also quote. My hope is that you will find your freedom to choose what you need on this journey and apply it to your life.

I am grateful for all those who have been beside me on this journey. I want to thank my spiritual community and the love and care I have received by participating and leading such a diverse group of people. It has been through their encouragement and response to my teachings that I have been able to learn so much about sharing practical application lessons each week.

I say a special thanks to Paul DeLanoit who has lead me through so many technical minefields that I had no idea how to navigate. Your part in this project has been invaluable and your work will shine around and through the words.

Thank you to all who helped to shape these words through reading the manuscript and giving valuable feedback: Rev. Charles Coppinger, Rose Frankfort, David Henson, Dorian Kreiling, Melinda Murphy and Virginia Van Horn.

Steve Schemmel has edited my manuscript and offered invaluable suggestions concerning content as well as grammatical and textual flow. My thanks to Steve for all the time and effort you have given and your encouraging words about getting this message out there.

A special thanks to Richard Tally for all his encouragement and suggestions in regard to this project. I can always count on Richard to have an opinion and help me think through anything that comes into my life.

And, thanks to my partner, Donald Johnson-Kidder, for believing in this project years before it even began. Thank you for designing the cover and knowing just exactly what I was wanting. Thank you for believing in the message and the messenger.

CHAPTER 1
Freedom, Anyone?

Freedom brings to mind so many different thoughts, but mostly they are thoughts that bring optimism and joy. Our own personal freedom, however, can be threatened by the prisons we build for ourselves, or the prisons we allow others to build for us. Prisons can include: lack of self-worth or self-esteem, health, the past, finances, religious background or religious abuse, sexual orientation, secrets, fear, self-expectations, the expectations of others, and more.

My purpose in writing this book is to help you examine your own personal freedom and the freedom of those around you. Together we will learn about freedom from our own prisons that keep us walled in and how they make us unable to really live our lives the way we want to live them.

In Luke 4:18, Jesus quotes Isaiah 61:1 when he says: "The spirit of God is on me, because God has anointed me to preach good news to the poor. God has sent me to proclaim freedom for the prisoners and recovery of sight for the blind and to release the oppressed." Jesus tells us here that bringing freedom was the main objective in his life. He applied this Old Testament text to himself. He made it public and was very clear that "freedom" was his call and mission in life.

Freedom Is More Than A Word or Concept

Personal Freedom is a Way of Life

Freedom in our lives must move beyond the lovely concepts of what freedom is or what freedom should be. It has to become a way of life for us…not a destination, but a journey of never-ending possibilities to find and practice freedom in our lives.

Many of us need to be set free from our suffering, our fears about being who we are, our fears of never being good enough or looking good enough, our fears of illness and death, our fears of being afraid, of never being able to please God, or God's vengeance around every corner, of our parents or of our economy.

In Galatians, the writer tells us: "When you did not know God, you were slaves to those who by nature are not gods. But now that you know God…how is it that you are turning back to those weak and miserable principles? Do you wish to be enslaved by them all over again?" (Galatians 4:8, 9)

We either have freedom in our lives or we are slaves to things, thoughts and attitudes and believe that people don't allow us to be free. Ultimately, it is our choice to be free or to be enslaved. Paul was telling the people in Galatia that they profess to know God and have the spirit of God in them, but they are turning back to their old ways of doing things. They were repeating their old ways of thinking and allowing themselves to again be enslaved—thus giving up their freedom. We cannot be free and, at the same time, live in a self-constructed prison.

We enslave ourselves over and over again when we build prisons that restrict and constrict our freedom until we are no longer free and become full-time prisoners. The choice is ours, although we would rather blame our imprisonment on others and play the victim.

Freedom From and Freedom To

When we talk about personal freedom in our lives, we have to talk about what we are free from and what our freedom gives us. We will need to examine what our freedom asks, requires and permits us to do. All of these are important topics that we will deal with in this book.

That Which We Fear
Has Great Power Over Us

Our fears of the present, our mistakes in the past and our concern about the future can all cause us to lose our freedom. Our personal fears have great power over us and will not allow us to move toward the freedom to be all that God is calling us to be.

Fear is the greatest inhibitor in our ability to exercise our freedoms in life. When fear is the controlling power in our lives, we become immobilized by our fears and again become prisoners.

When Jesus brought freedom to his world, it threatened the established religious authorities because it threatened their ability to control and exercise power over the people. Freedom is a threat to people who cannot handle freedom in their own lives. It is also a threat to the people who want to maintain power and authority over other people's lives. Jesus not only lived freedom but taught others how to have freedom. To do so was one of the most threatening stances he could take in his life. It is for us, as well.

Giving ourselves and others freedom can produce fear and anxiety for ourselves and others. Fear and anxiety come when we look at freedom as optional and not mandatory in our lives.

Freedom involves freedom from our own fears of inadequacy, self-esteem, job loss, illness, death, poverty, failure, God, religion, and more. It also involves moving forward exercising our freedom in ways that allow us to be free. Only then can we see the light of day and exercise our freedom no matter what is going on around us.

Contemporary author Harriet Ruben said: "Freedom is actually a bigger game than power. Power is about what you can control. Freedom is about what you can unleash." I think this is the greatest challenge of freedom—letting go and trusting. It means letting go of "holding your breath" in life and trusting in the freedom to just be you.

As Jesus stated in Luke 4:18, it was his calling and intention to bring freedom to the people he touched. He brought freedom in understanding a new and free relationship with God. It was not one based on the fear of a vengeful God, but of a loving, caring relationship with God's presence working good things in each person's life. He also brought freedom by healing people's physical, mental and emotional lives by giving them back what they had lost through fear, pain and death.

His words, his touch, his life, his every encounter challenged those he confronted to find and embrace freedom. Many accepted his call to freedom. Most of the people he encountered, however, were fearful of embracing something they could not imagine was even possible.

We often think that developing our spiritual lives causes us bondage. In reality, growing in our spiritual lives will produce spiritual freedom.   We must move from a passive, dependent role in our spiritual lives and our quest for freedom to an active, creative one.

When we are listeners and practitioners of others' spiritual direction, theology and mandates in our lives, we sell out our own responsibility and privilege of knowing God in our own way and on our own terms. I bought into a fundamentalist understanding of the Bible for many years in my spiritual journey. This gave me a very narrow and exclusive understanding of God and the world. When I finally took my own responsibility for my own spiritual journey, I had to find out on my own what I really believed. It became a freedom from a prison I had built for myself but I was unaware of it until I started looking for the key to get out.

It is easy to let others make our spiritual decisions and directions for us. We will never know personal freedom in our relationship with God when we abdicate the throne of our own personal experience and ability to know God personally.

This book will help you find freedom in your life that, I believe, you long for so strongly. I will share with you my own personal journey and the places where I have had to find freedom for myself. You will learn what it really takes to find and exercise freedom in your own life and allow others to have their freedom.

We do not trust ourselves with the freedom that God offers to us. When we are able to effect freedom in our own lives, we will have no need to deny freedom to anyone around us. When we give one another freedom, we begin to learn how to live as adults. The hardest thing about accepting our own freedom to be ourselves is that we must give freedom to others to allow them to realize their own freedom.

Emancipation Proclamation

"The Emancipation Proclamation was an executive order issued by United States President Abraham Lincoln on January 1, 1863, during the American Civil War under his war power. It proclaimed the freedom of 3.1 million of the nation's 4 million slaves, and immediately freed 50,000 of them, with the rest freed as Union armies advanced......," (Eric Foner). "Total abolition of slavery was finalized by the Thirteenth Amendment which took effect in December, 1865." (Wikipedia)

Emancipation defined is to be free from restraint, control, or the power of another, to be free from bondage, to be free from any controlling influence such as traditional mores or beliefs.

Just as the Emancipation Proclamation eventually freed slaves who had become prisoners, we can also write and exercise our own Emancipation Proclamation in our individual lives. Our personal Emancipation Proclamation can have the impact of changing our lives from slavery and being prisoners to being able to live our lives in freedom.

To emancipate and be emancipated we must first be able to understand what those things are that keep us from being free. To identify them and to move to release them and emancipate ourselves becomes one of the greatest tasks in our lives. It is one of the most important foundational steps we can ever take.

There are 10 steps that I will be expounding upon in this book. These are the 10 steps to your own, personal Emancipation Proclamation:

1. **I will move out of my prisons.**

2. **I will tear down the walls.**

3. **I will commit to build no more prisons for myself or for others.**

4. **I will not let others build prisons for me.**

5. **I will pursue my dreams unhindered by fear, negative opinions and my own dream inhibitors.**

6. **I will empower my dreams with my own freedom.**

7. **I will give freedom to others as I learn to give it to myself.**

8. **I will be the guardian of dreams not of prisons.**

9. I will remember that my dreams are important to the world.

10. I will encourage freedom of thought, freedom of expression and freedom to be.

These 10 steps, acted upon in your life, can truly set you free to become the person you have always wanted to be and to be all that God has created you to be.

"For to be free is not merely to cast off one's chains, but to live in a way that respects and enhances the freedom of others." (Nelson Mandela)

I am so glad that you are making a commitment to freedom, to learning more about it, to learning how to live it, how to break the limiting thoughts and actions that keep you from being free and learn to offer freedom to others so they can grow and become who they are created to be. My hope is that through this journey you will learn to live a life of freedom by learning to move out of your prisons, find your freedom (emancipation) and really start living.

CHAPTER 2
Prison Break

The first step in declaring our own personal Emancipation Proclamation is in making the decision that:

---

1. I WILL MOVE OUT OF MY PRISONS

Each of us wants to get rid of so much that would keep us from moving forward. It seems that those things keep reappearing in our lives and keep us from doing what we really want to do. These are the very things that keep us from being who we really want to be.

When we talk about the prisons in our lives, we are really talking about the structures that we have built in our minds and into our lives that keep us locked up and unable to move forward the way we want. Prisons are those places where we live that keep us away from our freedom. These prisons keep us locked up so that we cannot accomplish what we believe we are called to in life.

Each of us has personal prisons that we build. Then we lock the doors and hide the keys. We become victims to the prisons we build. Some of us proudly proclaim to the world: "I know I am in a prison of my own choosing and I am quite proud to live here." It will take more than recognizing our prisons. It will take a true desire to rid ourselves of our prisons and stop acting like the victims that we truly have chosen to be.

So, what are the prisons you have built in your own life—those fortresses that seem so confining yet add a certain amount of comfort to your life?

Identifying My Prisons

The first step in any movement forward toward freedom and healing always begins with identifying the problem(s).

In the New Testament, the writer in 2 Peter 2:19 says: "People are slaves to whatever has mastered them." (NRSV)

The Apostle Paul describes this slavery or imprisonment in different terms in Romans 7:23: "In every part of me I discover something fighting against my mind, and it makes me a prisoner of sin that controls everything I do." (CEV)

So we see here that we build our prisons because something is controlling us. We become prisoners to those things that control everything we do. We may say that we don't want to be a prisoner, but we have been in our prisons so long that we have a certain comfort level living there. Some of us have decorated our prisons and painted them such nice colors. We don't want to leave all the hard work that has gone into making our prisons so comfortable.

Every one of us has things in our lives that we can justify as legitimate prisons in our own lives. I have a list of my own concerns that could become my prisons: coming from small-town USA, fundamentalism, HIV, heart disease, cancer, fear, loneliness, self-esteem, anger, family and friends.

Communities feel justified in building prisons from what is happening or has happened in their lives: oppression, AIDS, breast cancer, prejudice, sexism, finances, education. We become victims to these things and give them power over us. They keep us from breaking out of our prisons because we have built those prisons and refuse to move out of them. We feel powerless when, in reality, we are the decision-makers about our prisons and about living in them.

What are <u>your</u> personal prisons you have built and are living in? Can you—will you—identify and name your prisons as a start on your healing journey?

When I use the excuse that I live in a prison and can't get freed from it, in essence, I am saying that I am choosing to live in prison. I am saying that I am not making the choice to move out of the prison and give myself freedom to truly be me. Identifying and naming my prisons must be the first step to knowing that I have them and finding the ways to get rid of them. Some of us can't even get past this step to be able to begin the healing process.

Finding The Keys

The interesting thing about prisons that we build for ourselves is that we are the only ones who have the keys. The prisons we have built for ourselves have the lock on the inside only. No one on the outside can ever lock or unlock your prison doors because you are the one who built your prison. You are the one who locked the door from the inside.

No one can lock me into my prisons. They are mine. I have made the decision to build them. I have been the architect and the contractor.

To paraphrase Hebrews 12:1: "We must get rid of everything that slows us down, especially our prisons that we won't destroy. And we must be determined to run the race that is ahead of us."

Living with challenges, hurts, angers, illnesses, disappointments and losses is the normal stuff of life. However, these can become prisons for us if we choose to build them on these foundations. Expectations of ourselves and expectations of others (including our family and friends) are also parts of life that can become prisons for us.

They only become our prisons when we lock ourselves and our feelings away and hide the keys. We become isolated and refuse to open the doors to let in the freshness of renewal, repentance, forgiveness, assistance and freedom.

Getting rid of everything means that we must locate the keys to our prisons and unlock the doors. Confinement is the key experience of living in prison. Moving about freely and going where we want to go freely only happens when we find the keys to unlock those prisons and leave them behind. Freedom to be all we are called to be can never happen from the confines of a prison.

There may be a number of factors that can help you find the keys: books, videos, therapists, insights, sacred writings, teachings, meditation, speakers, friends, spiritual communities and more. This book is one of the keys you can use. Only you can truly find the keys used to lock your prison doors. Only then can you walk out of your prisons, squinting at the sun, determined to move on.

Freedom is very frightening and scary...you are moving to a place that you may never have lived before. You may see things and experience things you would never have experienced in your prison.

The keys are there with you in your prisons. You have the ability to open every prison door and walk out. Only you can find your freedom to be who you are called to be. We pretend that we do not know where the keys are because we have become so comfortable in our walled fortresses. We have learned to live life not really trusting anything or anyone outside those doors.

Prison breaks only happen when we become engaged in our own freedom. The promise of freedom and others encouraging us to escape will never mean anything unless we are willing to change our lives from being prisoners to becoming free people.

Moving Out

Finding the keys is one thing. Moving out is a far different thing. Just finding the keys does not mean that you will use them. Some of us have gone to counselors or gotten good advice from friends or loved ones, or even attended church all our lives. All of that is helpful, but we, ourselves, are the ones who must physically and emotionally use the keys to unlock the doors before anything can begin to happen.

Finding the keys could mean that you just want to take a few excursions out of prison occasionally. Then you want to be able to flee back inside the walls of your self-imposed, false security. Moving out means taking up residence in another place: a place of freedom and light.

Darkness in our prisons always hides the ugliness and terror of our prisons. Finding the keys, opening the door and moving out will mean that our life will now be under the scrutiny of daylight. We will definitely have to deal with those things that could cause us to turn around and run headlong back into our prison. There we did not have to face any of the hobgoblins of our lives. We just let them continue to imprison us. To move out of prison means that we have taken the first step to live in a world that calls us to accountability, new growth and dealing with things as they come up. It will take a strong commitment not to open up that prison door and go back inside.

W Mitchell is a man who has truly found the keys to his potential prisons and moved on. He was in a blazing motorcycle accident and a paralyzing crash four years later. He has learned to take responsibility for the countless changes in his life. This former Marine is now sentenced to a lifetime in a wheelchair. He said: "The universe starts in your head and spreads out into the world. Change what happens in your head, and the universe changes."

When we live in our prisons of doubt, fear and insecurity we give away our power and ability to stand up for who we are. We give "them" the power to drive us back into our prisons and become recluses from what we know to be true about ourselves. Or, in many cases, we have no clue what is the truth about ourselves. We become prisoners of our doubt, fear and insecurity and we have never ventured out.

When we move out of our prisons, we may feel some temporary insecurity and doubts about staying out of our prisons. But, when we can be determined that our prisons are no longer where we want to live, we will begin to find that freedom to be and become.

For many of us, this seems to be an ongoing, lifetime struggle. It seems the longer we are locked away, the more difficult it is to keep from retreating back to our comfort zone. It can be like a criminal released from prison who returns to the crime that got him/her there in the first place because that is all (s)he knows.

Edgar J. Penn wrote these wonderful, poignant thoughts in a letter to a friend dated June 6, 1968:

"I am sad that Life seems to have such a hold on us all...or do we simply hold out our hands and say, 'Take me. Lead me. I need thus and so, and will not ask any questions.'

There are those, of course, who find the way for themselves; and no more tormented, lonely, suffering, besieged, and gloriously happy people are to be found, I think.

I would like to be able to say to Life: 'Never mind. I know the way from here.' And Life would be obliged to follow me for a change.

I feel I know the way, and yet, I am afraid. Afraid that perhaps, even though I may know the path, there may be a secret password, a nod, a wink, a knock which, my being ignorant of, would make my trek in vain.

And once having found myself at the Arch, I would have to stand there forever wondering what was on the other side, and yet, I would be with the few who could say, 'I found the way here alone.' That, in itself should warrant entry...and, who knows, perhaps it does."

Identify your prisons. Stop procrastinating and make a list. Find those keys that you have hidden away so securely and use them to unlock the door and release yourself from the darkness and solitary confinement in which you have placed yourself. Then, move out. Walk out into the sunshine of who you have always wanted to be without the locked prison doors and the shackles around your neck, hands and feet. Slam the door shut and leave it behind without fear of needing to return there again.

You hold it all in your hands. You can continue to be the prison builder, prison guard and keeper or you can choose to be completely freed from the prisons where you have insisted you want to live. Prisons are for those who have lost their freedom through choices they have made. Our personal freedoms can be lost in the same way—through the choices that we make.

You know what your prisons are—your mother, your father, your family, your illness, your fear, your thoughts of inadequacy, your anger, your spouse or lack thereof, your hurts, your background, your mistakes, your lost loves, your spiritual background, your refusal to grow up, your rationalizations, your lies, your prejudices, your traumas, your self-esteem, your feelings of worthlessness, your bad decisions, your fear of God, your judgments, your bad decisions—the list is endless.

All of us have reasons to build and live in prisons. The good news is that we don't have to. We built them. We hid the keys. We can find the keys. We can unlock the door. We can move out.

Viktor Frankl in his book, Man's Search for Meaning: Experiences in the Concentration Camp, sums up so well what this whole chapter has been about when he says: "Everything can be taken from a man (woman) but one thing: the last of the human freedoms—to choose one's attitude in any given set of circumstances, to choose one's own way. And there were always choices to make. Every day, every hour, offered the opportunity to make a decision, a decision which determined whether you would or would not submit to those powers which threatened to rob you of your very self, your inner freedom; which determined whether or not you would become the plaything of circumstance, renouncing freedom and dignity to become molded into the form of the typical inmate."

Step out into the world that is yours. Step out into the freedom of who you are called to be and not what everyone else thinks you should be. Find your freedom. Move out of your prison. Let your world know that you have found the keys and you're moving on.

CHAPTER 3
Wrecking Ball

---

2. I WILL TEAR DOWN THE WALLS OF MY PRISONS

"The world is full of lonely people, all isolated in a private, secret dungeon." Loretta Girzartis (American educator and writer).

We have become expertly adept at creating our own prisons and keeping the interiors beautifully appointed so that we feel very comfortable there. When we finally find the keys to unlock the door to our prisons and walk out of them, we might be tempted to keep our prisons available for later return. We might even want to work on the outside of our prisons, making them beautiful so that when we return, they will be a welcoming place to reside.

In moving out of our prisons, the next step is tearing down the walls. Getting rid of them may be the scariest and most threatening thing that we will ever do. To move out of our prisons and have the keys in our hands on the outside of the door is one thing. To actually dismantle the prisons we have lived in for so many years can actually threaten our stability and all of our security. It is not enough just to move out. We must be pro-active in tearing down those prisons so we cannot move back into them. Tearing them down means we can no longer go in and out of our prisons by placing a revolving door there.

Commitment

The first step we have to take is the commitment to actually tear our prisons down and destroy them. For many of us, this seems unlikely and sometimes next to impossible. We all think we have a special exemption from needing to tear down our prison walls. We truly believe that others just don't understand. We believe that someone else built the prisons we're in. We believe that our prisons are our existence. In many cases, it has become so comfortable in our prisons that we can't imagine moving out. We all have excuses for keeping those things in our lives that need to be thrown out and destroyed.

Romans 7:21-23 talks about this struggle: "I find this law at work: When I want to do good, evil is right there with me. For in my inner being I delight in God's law; but I see another law at work in the members of my body, waging war against the law of my mind and making me a prisoner of the law of sin (missing the target or bull's-eye) at work within my members."

The writer of Romans shows us the duality of the desire to move into freedom and the pull to keep on doing things the old way. As a result, we never find that freedom we're looking for.

Commitment to tearing down the walls of our prisons begins the minute we have walked out of our prisons and decide not to go back. Tearing down the prisons will be even a greater task than finding the keys we've hidden so well.

We found our security and our entire way of life while living in our prisons. We always want there to be an "escape" back into the prison just in case we need it. Some of us go back and forth, into and out of our prisons so easily that we don't even realize we're doing it. By being committed to tearing down the walls, we are making a decision that we will NOT go back into the prison because it's not there anymore.

1 Corinthians 5:7 states the following imperative: "Get rid of the old yeast that you may be a new batch without yeast—as you really are." "Get rid of" is the key phrase in this quote. We can keep the garbage and the unhealthy living spaces alive and well. We already know how to do that. The key to freedom comes in making a commitment to tearing down the walls of our prisons. After making that commitment, demolition may not begin immediately, but, if

we are committed to destroying the walls of our prisons, it will come to fruition.

Destroy

At some point, you have to begin demolition. Demolition is a huge task. It is dirty. It takes long hours and there are some risks involved when tearing down something you have taken so much care to build so strong. The prisons of our own makings have walls and walls inside of walls. They are usually surrounded by huge defensive walls and fences that we have built to keep our prisons and ourselves very well protected. Demolition will require more than one tool. It will involve the use of heavy equipment including a gigantic commitment to follow through to the very end.

Proverbs 1:32, 33 states: "For the waywardness of the simple will kill them, and the complacency of fools will destroy them; but whoever listens to me will live in safety and be at ease, without fear of harm." When we are able to step up to confront our prisons and begin to tear them down, we have a greater ability to tap back into that God presence and Christ consciousness. Then we are able to live in safety and be at ease, without fear of harm.

We have used our prisons as protection and insulation against all the "bad" things out there. We become hurt or disillusioned and we are holed up in our prisons. We become fearful about tearing them down. It will take picks, shovels, a wrecking ball, sledge hammers, heavy equipment and determination to rid ourselves of these prisons that have such a hold on our lives. We did not build them simply overnight and we will not be able to tear them down in just one day or one session. It was a gradual process building our prisons and it will not be easy to tear them down.

We may find that when we start tearing down our prison walls there will be more prisons to the right or the left of the current prison we are tearing down. We might even find a prison within our prison. It is a journey of discovery and freedom that will never be experienced until we find our freedom to move out of our prisons and then begin to destroy them forever.

Getting Rid Of Debris

When we are making some progress in tearing down the walls of our prisons, we have to begin to haul the rubbish away. If we don't, we will sort through the rubbish to find all those essential elements it took to build and maintain our prisons and we will hang on to these bits and pieces of that prison. We could even look for ways to rebuild that prison or use these stones and other ingredients to start another, new, prison.

Not only will we have to tear down the walls and haul away the debris, we must then get to work on the foundation. Ah, you thought I might not say something about the foundation because this chapter is about tearing down our walls. The foundation is next, then.

What caused you to build it in the first place: fear, hurt, anger, jealousy, sickness, job loss, family, lost love, lack of self worth, your sexuality, wrong decisions, others' opinions of you? These are all potential foundations to the prisons we have built. If we do not destroy the foundations, we will definitely, at some point in our lives, build another prison right there on the remains of that foundation.

In my own life, how did I move through finding out that I was HIV+ in 1987 when everyone told me I had 6 months to live? How have I survived in a large city when I came from such a small little place in the foothills of Appalachia? How have I remained true to the call that God has on my life when so much would come against me to try to convince me that I am doing the wrong thing or I just need to quit? I had to decide not to let these become prisons in my life and keep me from doing what I have been called to do.

All of us have this opportunity but it will take determination to:

1. Refuse to build prisons.

2. Search out help from wise people and apply that wisdom to my situation.

3. Take responsibility for my stuff, my beliefs about who I am and the world.

4. Make a commitment to tear down a prison that I can identify.

We all have places in our lives where we just want to sit down and let life pass on by. Determine not to be that person! We are not called to a passive life of sitting in prisons watching the world go by. We are called to a life of being active, involved and aggressive, living life that brings freedom and not imprisonment. We were created to live life without shackles and locks that keep us from moving into our freedom to be who we are called to be.

Psalm 30:11, 12: "You turned my wailing into dancing; you removed my sackcloth and clothed me with joy, that my heart may sing to you and not be silent." Here are the results of moving out of our prisons, tearing down the walls and completely destroying the foundation. It means not being bound up anymore and beginning life renewed and refreshed—walking in sunshine and breathing the freshness of freedom.

Tear down the walls of your prisons. There is no better time than the present to get busy on your prisons. Nobody else can or will help you to tear them down. They are your prisons. You are the architect, builder and warden. It also means that you have the right and responsibility to tear them down, haul away the rubbish and destroy the foundation. Every building that comes down that you have built means that you have more space in your life to live in freedom and at peace. It means not being confined to that which would destroy you.

How do you do that? It takes holding out your hand (in the space where your prison was) and grasping the hand of the universe—the power that wants you to succeed. The power to be your unique self that the world is waiting to see revealed.

When we bring in that wrecking ball we create space to live in freedom and peace, living in harmony with the Universe.

Romans 8:19: "Creation waits in eager expectation for the children of God to be revealed." For each one of us to be "revealed" we must move out of our prisons, tear down the walls, remove the rubbish, destroy the foundations and move into a free place, finding our journey has just begun—one more time.

CHAPTER 4
No More Building

We have talked about identifying our prisons, finding the keys to unlock our prisons and then moving out of our prisons. The second step we talked about is tearing down the walls of our prisons and destroying the foundations. The third step to writing our own Emancipation Proclamation is:

---

3. I WILL COMMIT TO BUILD NO MORE PRISONS FOR MYSELF OR FOR OTHERS

Identifying our prisons and destroying them will do no good to our growth process if we do not commit to stop building personal prisons. Some of us begin building new prisons even as we tear down the old one, selecting the same building blocks that we used in our previous prisons.

43

Commitment Is Key

A commitment is an agreement or pledge to do something. Why is it that we hesitate or refuse to make a commitment about our prisons? The biggest fear is that we will fail or be unable to keep the commitments we make. That fear is what we call the "human condition." We cannot foresee what the future may hold when we are making a commitment. However, we must step forward and make a commitment based upon all the information we have up to that point in time.

Making the commitment to stop building prisons for ourselves or others must take place at that specific point. It is like going to the first AA meeting or taking the first step in a weight-loss program. It will also involve a continuing commitment to make sure that we do not fall back into those comfortable and dangerous places that we love so much.

This commitment also involves a realization that as a master builder of prisons, you will move that knowledge and expertise into building your own life of freedom. It will also enable you to allow others to have that same freedom.

Determination Is Mandatory

Making up your mind is the first step. Determination is a resolve to keep the commitment you have made in regard to prisons. It follows as the ingredient that will keep that commitment front and center. Determination becomes the legs and the feet of the commitment to no longer build or live in prisons. A support team that is encouraging and to whom you can be accountable is also an important ingredient to making this determination work.

Commitment to not building prisons for ourselves or others is the goal we are striving to accomplish. Determination is the practical step to making that happen. It is what moves us forward even when the going gets tough. Often all we want to do is retreat to our prisons or rush to get another one built where we can "live" more comfortably. Our determination must kick in again and cause us to move away from those planning and thought processes that keep us from moving forward.

Permission Is NOT Granted

You cannot build a prison until you have planned it out and know exactly why you need to build it. When building plans arise from your fears, hurts, anxieties and people around you, you cannot give yourself permission to build new prisons. Others cannot build prisons in your life unless you give them permission. Yes, that makes you in control of your life. Many of us have just given over our lives to others who will run them and possibly ruin them.

We may make some mistakes in the decisions we make in our lives. Ultimately, we must take responsibility for those decisions. This also includes taking responsibility for the prisons we have built and those that may arise in the future.

When we refuse to approve plans and do not give permission for new prisons to be built, we will begin to learn the importance of "no" in our lives. We can embrace our commitment with strength and confidence saying: "I am ultimately in charge of my life and I can be strong enough to face life instead of hiding in my prison where I feel safe."

We want so much for all of our problems and challenges to be someone else's fault. That way, we can blame them and we can play the victim and the martyr.

Linda Forrest in her book, The Faces of Victim, says: "Victims deny both their problem-solving abilities and their potential for self-generated power. Instead they tend to see themselves as too fragile to handle life. Feeling done in by, at the mercy of, mistreated, intrinsically bad and wrong, they see themselves as the 'un-fixable problem'."

When we dwell in our prisons and become the victim to other people, our family or circumstances in our lives, we become a person that becomes powerless. We end up giving permission to these people or our circumstances to build prisons for us and we give ourselves permission to, again, hide inside them.

No one, including you, can ever build a prison without your permission. When you realize that, you are taking responsibility for either building your own prisons or giving permission to others to build a prison for you. Taking responsibility for your own life and for all the successes and failures that will come from just living life is what it means to be an adult. You are then no longer able to blame everything that comes at you as the events that allow you to build your prisons. Many of us just want to be children all our lives. We allow ourselves to be tossed around by every wind that comes along. We are "just the victim" to everything that "just happens" to us in our lives.

James 1:2-4 says: "Consider it pure joy, my friends, whenever you face trials of many kinds, because you know that the testing of your faith develops perseverance. Perseverance must finish its work so that you may be mature and complete, not lacking anything."

Changing Vocations Must Happen

We must change our vocation from being prison builders and guardians to being the architects and guardians of our dreams. We must be determined to do whatever it takes to stop being the builder of our own prisons. We must take responsibility not to build any more prisons for ourselves or others. No matter who builds your prisons, you or others, you still hold the keys in your hand and you can set yourself free.

We stay in our prisons because of insecurity, refusal to take responsibility, laziness, indecisive behavior, refusing to grow up. We like being the victim; we feel safe and secure.

You <u>can</u> grow and become all you are created to be when you move out of your prisons and refuse to build more prisons. Moving about freely in life, instead of living in confinement, allows us the ability to take our lives back and live fully.

Prisons become hell for many of us. We have already determined that life will not be happy. We have been hurt, bruised and battered. We believe our only chance of surviving is by going inside our walls and keeping everyone and everything out. Bishop Carlton Pearson writes the following in his book, The Gospel of Inclusion: "We are begging for freedom through bondage. But freedom is not for cowards. We must thrust our lives into the hands of the living God whom we cannot see and trust God to secure our future. This security must not be built upon our system of ideologies that control, limit and deceive us."

We are created and called to be free. We are created to walk around in open spaces of freedom and love, not to be confined in prisons we or others have built.

We must begin the freedom process by committing to not building more prisons for ourselves or allow others to build them for us. Only people who have become so adept at building their own prisons can also be the experts to build prisons for others. We must stop the building process that only limits and punishes. We must be the givers of life to others and allow them the freedom to be all they can be. We must make a commitment to stop building those prisons and commit to follow through.

When Nehemiah (in the First Testament of the Bible) spoke to the leaders of Jerusalem about God calling him to rebuild the walls of the city and to restore the city, the people replied "Let us start rebuilding."

Every moment of every day we have the opportunity to begin rebuilding our lives. It makes no difference if you're 20 or 200 years old. The opportunity to make a commitment to stop building more prisons for yourself must be made.

You can be the architect of your future. A future of freedom and power. A future of becoming the best that you can be. It begins with tearing down and destroying. It continues with making a commitment to stop building what you know so well. That only ends up imprisoning you. You must be willing to go forward in building freedom structures in your life. You must make the new structures of your life healthy living spaces filled with light and freedom.

Stop building prisons for yourself and for others. Pull all the permits currently open for building prisons and burn them. Begin, then, to rebuild your life, minus the prisons. Take the power and control that allows you to move forward into the place of freedom that God is calling you. Soon you will forget how to build prisons and celebrate building a life of openness, joy, peace and freedom.

CHAPTER 5
Just Say 'NO'

4. I WILL NOT LET OTHERS BUILD PRISONS FOR ME

We all have prisons that we have allowed others to build in our lives. We have given them permission and stood by while they worked very hard to imprison us with their thoughts, judgments, expectations, words and actions.

Matthew 12:25, 29: "Every kingdom divided against itself will be ruined, and every city or household divided against itself will not stand...How can anyone enter a strong person's house and carry off their possessions unless that person first ties up the strong person? Then that person's house can be robbed."

We become divided when others build prisons for us. Our lives become divided into multi-factions when people put us into their prisons. Jesus teaches that a person who is divided will be ruined and will not stand. We allow others to tie us up and rob us of our freedom and to take away everything that truly makes us unique. Here is the greatest place in our lives where we could play the martyr. It is here that we want to believe that we have no responsibility when others build prisons for us. Ultimately, though, it is our decision to allow others to build prisons for us.

How They Build

So, how do others build prisons in our lives to imprison us and rob us of our very essence?

1. *Religion*

Some of us are still in prisons built by our parents or other family members, church authorities and even the Bible.

Matthew 20:25 states: "Jesus called them together and said, 'You know that the rulers of the Gentiles lord it over them, and their high officials exercise authority over them.'" We can reside in a prison of interpretation, religious nonsense and fear. This can be a prison of our own building or one built by others. Religion is merely mankind's attempt to understand God. It is not the "be all and end all" to knowing God personally. We have allowed religion, religious zealots (fanatics and fundamentalists), self-proclaimed authorities and others' interpretations to rule our lives. We have given up our freedom to understand God in our own unique way and experience.

2. *Family*

Some of us have allowed family to build prisons for us. Many of us fear telling the world who we truly are because of "what the family would think." We have allowed their opinions and power to build a prison and put us into it. We have allowed family to dictate who we are and how we live.

Family can also build prisons in our lives because they want everyone in the family to do it their way. They even pull the "parent, older, wiser, financial (including the will) card" and we let them.

3. _Expectations_

When we allow others' expectations to rule us, we are giving over our lives to those who want to tell us how to live them. Others expect us to be a certain way or act a certain way and we give in. We, then, become imprisoned in their web of actions and reactions. We give them the power to tell us who we should be and how we should act. We allow ourselves to become imprisoned by running around trying to make everyone happy.

4. _Shame And Guilt_

Shame and guilt come from our friends, family, church, society, school, jobs, government and many other outside forces. It is an attempt to get us back into the rut of living according to someone else's definition and direction. When we truly believe that we are a bad person or someone who cannot make good decisions, we live with the shame and guilt that others want to impose upon us. We allow ourselves to be manipulated and castigated because we are convinced that we are not a worthy person and we need to be confined and punished.

5. *Failures And Successes*

We allow ourselves to be imprisoned by our own failures and successes and what others think about them (or what we think they think about them). We nurse, curse and rehearse our failures while others are building a prison because of our failings. We move right into that prison because we never want to move away from our failures and get on with our lives.

Even our successes can become a prison that others build for us because they are jealous. They don't want to hear that we have been successful. They want to punish us for being successful when they are not experiencing their own success. Ben Sweetland (author) said: "Success is a journey, not a destination." We must not allow the prison of failures or successes to be built in our lives and stop us from moving forward to try the "next thing" in our lives.

Why They Build

People build prisons in our lives for various reasons. Many of those reasons have to do with manipulation and perceived power to get what they want from you.

1. *Desire For Power*

The number one reason people build prisons in others' lives is so that they can have power over another person. Sometimes people are so powerless in their own lives that they propose to build prisons in others' lives. That way, they can have power over somebody. Power over another gives them the ability to become the warden of a prison. It makes them feel as if they look better and they believe they are better than those in prisons.

The religious leaders of Jesus' day used their knowledge of religion to lord it over everyone else. Jesus called them "whitewashed tombs" which look beautiful on the outside but on the inside are just a bunch of dead bones.

2. *Manipulation*

People use their perceived power to manipulate and get their way. Once a person is put into a prison another has built for them, they can be manipulated and controlled. The builder and warden now have ultimate power. We have given away our own personal freedom and power. We must acknowledge our own responsibility for allowing others to manipulate and potentially ruin our lives.

We gripe and complain about these people in our lives that continually tell us what to do and who to be. In the end, we have given them permission to act the way they do and we continue to give them more and more power.

3. *Ignorance*

Sometimes people build prisons in our lives out of their own ignorance. They may not "know any better," as we say, and may speak to us through their own ignorance on spirituality or how to live. We listen to them instead of our own hearts. Most of the time our hearts tell us that they don't know what they're talking about. However, we still let them instill fear and power over us. Then they end up building prisons for us and we sit down and begin to wring our hands. We can make our own decisions and we <u>can</u> discern a person's motives and manipulations. It is then that we must decide to make our own decisions in regard to what is best for us in our lives.

Stop The Building

Only you have the ability to demand that someone else stop building prisons in your life. No amount of perceived power on the other's part can ever allow them to build a prison in your life unless you have given them permission.

1. *Just Say "No"*

This is one of the hardest things we have to do in our lives. We want everyone to like us. We want to be like everyone else instead of standing out as a true individual. We just don't want to rock the boat. Just say "No" to others building prisons in your life. It starts by saying it out loud: "I hear what you're saying about how I should do this, but I am not you and I need to do it my way, whether I fail or succeed." It begins with just a simple "no" and then following through to move in your own direction.

2. *Take Back Your Power*

When you allow someone else to build a prison in your life, you have given away your power. You have told them they have a right to invade your life and to build whatever it is they want to build. You have moved off the throne of your life and given that power over to someone else. Taking our power back means saying "no" and it means living a life unhampered by the manipulations and power takeovers by those in our lives.

3. *Remember Your Dreams*

Our power comes from remembering our dreams. When we are imprisoned, we are unable to live our dreams. Our ability to move about in freedom is hampered and chained. We are living a life that is dictated by others. Our prisons keep us from being who we really are and accomplishing the dreams that are ours exclusively. Remembering our dreams means going back to that vision and drive to be who we are called to be and to accomplish that which we know to be our calling.

4. *Move Out, Tear Down, Destroy*

So, the final thing we will have to do with these prisons that others have built in our lives is the same thing that we have to do with the prisons we have built for ourselves: Move out, tear them down and destroy them.

It begins by opening your eyes to the fact that you do have prisons that others have built for you. They come from their false authority, manipulation and ignorance. You <u>can</u> be who you are called to be. You <u>can</u> be the one in charge of your life and be all that you can be.

The task to remove these prisons from your life may even be bigger than tearing down the prisons you have built for yourself. You may hurt the prison warden's feelings. You may lose a friend in your life, or even a family member.

It happens when you identify the prisons and who has built them. It means making a conscious effort to move out of them, to tear them down and to destroy them. It also demands close monitoring so that others are not allowed (by you) to build new prisons for your life. Take back your power. Move out of those prisons and find you for the very first time.

Galatians 5:1 states: "It is for freedom that we have been set free. Stand firm then, and do not let yourselves be burdened again by a yoke of slavery." (paraphrase)

CHAPTER 6
Flying Fearlessly

---

5. I WILL PURSUE MY DREAMS UNHINDERED BY FEAR, NEGATIVE OPINIONS AND MY OWN DREAM INHIBITORS

Step number five has to do with the pursuit of our dreams and how we move forward. Of course, moving forward involves the first four steps we have talked about concerning finding the freedom to move out of our prisons.

This step on our path to personal freedom can be a place of great progress and forward movement. It can also be a stopping place where we choose not to move forward in order to fly. We find that we know what our dreams are, but we are unable to get them accomplished. This happens because of a number of different things that get in our way and hinder us from pursuing our dreams.

1 Timothy 6:20 states: "Guard what has been entrusted to your care. Turn away from godless chatter and the opposing ideas of what is falsely called knowledge."

Paul warns Timothy that he must be careful not to give in to "godless chatter and opposing ideas." Today's English Version says: "profane talk and foolish arguments." The Contemporary English Version says: "godless and stupid talk that sounds smart but really isn't." The Living Bible says: "godless mixture of contradictory notions." All of these are ways of saying that people and the voices in your own head will be calling out foolish arguments and talk that has nothing to do with your ultimate direction in your life.

To be able to successfully fly fearlessly, we must take charge of what we hear or what we invent in our own minds and move forward with the fulfillment of our dreams.

Unhindered By Fear

Fear is the greatest factor that can ruin our journey to accomplish our dreams. We fear what others will think. We fear failure. We fear success. We fear how hard the journey will be to realize our dreams. We fear being misunderstood, laughed at or the possibility of standing out from others.

Fear is an emotional response to a perceived threat. Note here that it is not necessarily something that is real but something that is "perceived." Not all fear is bad, but fear is dangerous when it causes us to shut down and stop moving forward to realize our dreams. We give in to our fears by not pursuing our dreams, not keeping them alive and doing what it takes to make them come to fruition. Fear can motivate us or it can stop us dead in our tracks. It is the biggest and most crippling of all the reasons we choose to stay in our prisons instead of moving out of them to pursue our dreams.

We must commit to overcome the fear that would easily entrap us and keep us immobilized. We cannot move forward while being gagged and chained by fear and remaining in a prison of fear where we have misplaced our keys.

Unhindered By Negative Opinions

This refers not only to others' negative opinions, but ones that we, ourselves, have.

2 Timothy 2:16 says: "Avoid godless chatter, because those who indulge in it will become more and more ungodly." Godless chatter sets us up to have our dreams locked down and we become unable to fly. It is chatter that can take place in our own head and through conversations with others. There is a great push in our world for everyone to toe the mark and keep the status quo.

There are many negative opinions out there when it comes to fighting for your dreams. Getting good advice from an individual or a group of people can be a very good thing.

It can also become a bunch of negative opinions and stop you from moving forward.

We can become confused and immobilized when we have no idea how to screen what others are saying when they give advice. Proverbs 13:10 tells us: "Wisdom is found in those who take advice." Our greatest challenge is discerning the advice and opinions that will come our way in relationship to our dreams.

There are always many negative opinions to go around. Our task then becomes finding a way to dismiss those and move forward. The negative opinions can stop us from realizing our dreams or they can truly spur us forward with a greater determination to realize and make our dreams come true.

Unhindered By My Own Dream Inhibitors

Some of us don't have to get thwarted by others' negative opinions. We can sabotage ourselves without anyone else's help. Our own issues (our prisons) that we refuse to deal with can be the very reasons why we cannot move forward to release ourselves to live our dreams.

1. *Self-Worth*

We can either think too lowly of ourselves or too highly of ourselves. Both can keep us from flying high with our dreams. Our self-worth and our understanding of what a unique creation we are is a key to moving forward instead of standing still or going backwards. Our self-worth may be influenced by parents, teachers, religion or other outside influences. In the end, each of us has to take responsibility for finding our unique spot in all of creation and use that to our advantage to be all that we can be.

2. _Insecurities_

Our insecurities become dream inhibitors because they cause us to never want to risk or take a chance. Our insecurities come from inside of us and speak to us in loud and demanding voices. They say, "You cannot do this." "You will fail and people will not like you." "You have no idea what you're doing." "You're not qualified." "Somebody smarter or more skilled should be doing this, not you." We believe these voices and insecurities and we give in and stop moving forward. Our insecurities leave us feeling less than enthused and less inspired to move ahead.

3. _Laziness_

Being all that we can be takes a lot of energy and work. Let's face it, some of us are just too lazy to make it happen. It's so much easier not to swim against the tide, or open new vistas and break new ground. It's so much easier to live life as we've always lived it and not rock the boat. Swimming against the tide involves building up your muscles so that you can continue moving forward no matter what might come your way. It means making a conscious decision to move forward and then moving the obstacles out of the way to make it happen. Laziness gets in the way of dreams being built and lived.

4. *Disorganization*

Some of us are so disorganized and strung-out that we could never move in a new direction because it would take so much work to get ourselves organized that we would be dead before that could happen. We let disorganization and the lack of making decisions ruin our chances of moving forward. We look at all that we would have to do to clean up the mess around us and then we miss out on charging forward because we have too much stuff around us that would hinder us from rising up to fly.

5. *Procrastination*

Well, there is always tomorrow. That's the greatest excuse and lie that we tell ourselves about realizing and living our dreams. Procrastination is a handy device to deceive ourselves. It causes us to believe we can wait just one more hour or one more day or one more year to get things together to work our dreams. Can you imagine what would happen in our world if everyone stopped procrastinating and got the thing done that needs to be done? It's a matter of starting the project, gathering information, making the right contacts and drawing the plans. It takes moving forward, moving forward, moving forward. Procrastination becomes one of the greatest weights around our necks holding us back.

I Will Pursue My Dreams

The word "pursue" means "to follow in order to overtake, capture, defeat, to engage in." A synonym for "pursue is "chase." Do you see all the action words in that definition? Our dreams do not just float by like a cloud and then we jump up and capture them and they get fulfilled. When we say, "I will pursue my dreams," it means that it will take energy and planning to overtake, capture and engage. It will mean that I will chase those dreams up, down and sideways to make them come true.

Philippians 3:12-14 says: "I press on to take hold of that for which God took hold of me. I do not consider myself yet to have taken hold of it. But one thing I do: Forgetting what is behind and straining toward what is ahead, I press on toward the goal to win the prize for which God has called me." The Phillips Translation states it this way: "I forget all that lies behind me and with hands outstretched to whatever lies ahead I go straight for the goal."

That's the picture of flying fearlessly.

CHAPTER 7
Free To Be

6. I WILL EMPOWER MY DREAMS WITH MY OWN FREEDOM

When we understand that freedom is really what God has given us, we are able to extend that same freedom to everyone else that we encounter. When I don't have freedom to be who I am, I have no ability to give you the freedom to be who you are. When I don't want you to have your freedom, then I do whatever I can to take it away from you.

1 Peter 2:16 states: "As servants of God, live as free people." Our life dreams and freedom will only come when we grasp the concept that we can empower our own dreams with our own freedom. Finding our freedom to be who we

truly are gives us the ability to accomplish our dreams in our way, in our own time and place.

Don Riso, in his book, <u>Personality Types</u>, states: "Through the process of honestly seeking the truth about ourselves, we gradually transform ourselves from who we are into who we can be, into persons who are fuller, more life affirming and self-transcending. When we get stuck in the part of who we are and telling the truth about who we are, we cannot have freedom."

To Be Or Not To Be, That Is The Question

We struggle with giving ourselves permission to be who we truly are and to act upon our unique place in this world. Empowering our dreams can only come with exercising our freedom to be. When we are imprisoned by anything or anyone, we are thwarted in moving forward to realize our dreams.

Ephesians 4:15 says: "Speaking the truth in love, we will in all things grow up." Guess what freedom is all about. Growing up!! Growing up is the slow process of learning to tell oneself the truth. The most important step in freedom is to be our own truth-tellers about our own truth. It means being able to tell the truth about who I am right now. I may not be that same person a week from now, or a year from now or even five years from now. However, I have the freedom to be who I am right now in this place and time. That's the truth-telling about who I am and where I am on my journey. It is also about where I've been. It takes introspection, it takes inspection, and it takes the truth about who I am.

When we can't tell the truth about others, we can't tell the truth about ourselves. We need to be able to have the truth, be the truth, tell the truth and live the truth every day of our lives. Freedom will never come until we find our truth and until we speak it and live it. It includes our habits, our thoughts, our faults, our strong and weak points, failures and successes and all of our struggles. John Joseph Powell in Why Am I Afraid to Tell You Who I Am? says: "The greatest kindness that I ever have to offer you is always the truth."

When we cannot see truth, we build a wall or a prison. Our light has been turned off and it limits our freedom. We don't have the ability to move forward to all that we can be.

Being A Freedom-Giver And A Freedom-Receiver

Matthew 10:8 says: "Freely you have received, freely give." As we receive our own freedom from ourselves and God, we learn more and more about giving it to others. Some of us are really hung up about giving freedom and getting freedom from other people.

The greatest journey we can make is to be freed from our prisons. We can't just walk out, tear down the walls and destroy the foundation. We must also be able to move on in our lives where our prisons are no longer the center of our existence.

Making freedom a journey and not a goal means learning how to be responsible for our own freedom and not allowing others to imprison us again. We will make mistakes in the process of learning to give and receive freedom, but we must push forward to be good in both giving and receiving.

Proverbs 4:18: "The path of the righteous is like the first gleam of dawn, shining ever brighter till the full light of day." Freedom is a journey, not a destination. This passage reminds us that it starts out like that little, tiny spark of light and then it shines brighter and brighter.

Neale Donald Walsch in <u>Conversations with God</u> puts it this way: "So long as you are still worried what others think of you, you are owned by them. Only when you require no approval from outside yourself can you own yourself." God gives me the approval. God says, "I made you and I'm proud of you right where you are."

1 Peter 2:9-10: "You are a chosen people, a royal priesthood, a holy nation, a people belonging to God, that you may declare the praises of God who called you out of darkness into wonderful light. Once you were not a people, but now you are the people of God."

Knowing Who God Is Means I Can Know Who I Am

2 Corinthians 3:17, 18: "Now the Lord is the spirit, and where the spirit of the Lord is, there is freedom. And we, who with unveiled faces all reflect the Lord's glory are being transformed into God's likeness with ever-increasing glory, which comes from God, who is the Spirit."

It is the spirit of God in me that gives me the freedom to be who I am. The first freedom comes when we understand that we have the Spirit of God in us. We can share that with others and vice versa. I must be able to see God in everything and everyone around me to be able to become an "unveiled face"—not confined by my own God in a box, but allowing others to know God in different ways than I do.

We are truly being transformed to reflect the very face of God. John Joseph Powell reminds us in his book: "I can help you to accept and open yourself mostly by accepting and revealing myself to you." I can give you the freedom to be who you are just by being me!

It is the freedom to be, which becomes the power to be, which becomes the freedom to be, which becomes the power to be. It goes in a circle.

Our freedom is the breeding ground and the fruition of our dreams. We are hampered and halted in making our dreams come true when we refuse to accept the freedom of God to be just who we are. We must stop buying cheap dreams from others and begin lavishly producing our own dreams. We find freedom from our prisons through being reminded who God is and who we are.

Psalm 119:45: "I will walk about in freedom for I have sought out your precepts." Walking in freedom allows us to be free to pursue our dreams, fueled by our freedom. It causes us to be able to give others freedom to be who they are and to pursue their dreams.

My prayer for your freedom and your dreams comes from Proverbs 4:12: "When you walk, your steps will not be hampered; when you run, you will not stumble."

CHAPTER 8
Freedom For All

---

7. *I WILL GIVE FREEDOM TO OTHERS AS I LEARN TO GIVE IT TO MYSELF*

When we are able to give freedom away, we truly have freedom within ourselves. This is the freedom to be who we are, to "become," change, grow and live.

Why Don't We Give Freedom To Others?

1. *We Don't Want To Accept One Another*

Romans 15:5-7: "May the God who gives endurance and encouragement give you a spirit of unity among yourselves, so that with one heart and mouth you may glorify

God. Accept one another, then, just as Christ accepted you, in order to bring praise to God."

The whole bottom line about freedom is accepting one another. If I don't accept who you are, I'm not able to give you freedom to be who you are. And when I don't accept you, then I'm not able to give you freedom. In essence, I want you to become something different, or to do "it" a different way.

Accepting means that I don't use manipulation or coercion, guilt or pressure to have you conform to my understanding or my way of doing things. When we give someone else freedom, it becomes a gift and we can have no strings attached to it. A gift is not a gift if it still has strings attached. When you give freedom, you give freedom.

All of us have strings attached to our hearts concerning freedom. "Well, I can be free, but...."and there's the attachment. The big string is the big "but." It makes us hold back on who we really can be. If I cannot give myself freedom, I certainly will be unable to give that gift to someone else.

Thomas Moore in <u>Care of the Soul</u> says: "Soul respects another's failures to find perfection, resistance to enlightenment, sheer ignorance of absolute truth, misguided attachments and unrelenting meandering."

Freedom allows us to give other people the faith to be who they are, and to be at the place they need to be on their journey. Taking that freedom away from them also takes freedom away from ourselves.

2. *We Want To Judge Others*

We feel that we have the right to judge others. We become the judge, the jury and the executioner of other people's actions and lives. When we do that we crawl right up into the God chair and we take over as God. "I have now become God. I can read your motives. I can read your mind.

I can understand your actions. I'm going to be able to pass judgment on everything in your life."

Many times, the greatest problem we have in our relationships is that we are trying to get people to be what we want them to be. We are not happy that others don't look like us, act like us and don't say what we want them to say.

Romans 14:1-4: "Accept the person whose faith is weak, without passing judgment on disputable matters. One person's faith allows him/her to eat everything, but another person, because of their faith, eats just certain foods. The person who eats everything must not look down on the one who does not, and the person who does not eat everything must not condemn the person who does. Who are you to judge someone else?"

We judge one another because it makes us feel superior to everyone else. That's why we judge. That's not giving freedom—that's taking freedom away. When I become superior to you, you are always less than me. We must remember and practice the fact that we are walking side by side on this journey and no one is superior to the person beside them.

When we start judging people about where they are in their lives, their beliefs, their priorities, we step out of the side by side relationship and become God. When we withhold freedom because of our own insecurities and judge others negatively, we become afraid of our own freedom.

3. *We Want To Show Partiality*

1 Peter 4:8 states: "Above all, love each other deeply, because love covers over a multitude of sins." When we talk about sin we are talking about an archery term where one misses the bull's eye when shooting an arrow. When we want everyone around us to be like us, think like us, have the same priorities we do and exclude others from our lives based on these criteria, we are showing partiality or favoritism.

Romans 12:16-18 says: "Live in harmony with one another. Do not be proud, but be willing to associate with people of low position. Do not be conceited. Do not repay anyone evil for evil. Be careful to do what is right in the eyes of everybody. If it is possible, as far as it depends on you, live at peace with everyone."

4. *We Want To Show Favoritism*

James 2:1-4 says: "Don't show favoritism. Suppose a person comes into your meeting wearing a gold ring and fine clothes, and a poor person in shabby clothes also comes in. If you show special attention to the person wearing fine clothes and say, 'Here's a good seat for you,' but you say to the poor person, 'You stand there,' or 'Sit on the floor by my feet,' have you not discriminated among yourselves and become judges with evil thoughts?"

We might show favoritism or partiality based on a person's finances, hair color, sexual orientation, economic status or the way a person dresses, talks or has an accent, or their politics or lack thereof. When we show favoritism or partiality, we become the oppressor.

John J. McNeill in <u>Freedom, Glorious Freedom</u> states the following: "Pathological religion relies on fear of punishment to obtain obedience; it uses guilt as a subtle lever for manipulation and control. It fears freedom and cultivates blind, unquestioning obedience. Even normal doubts are punished and repressed because they are seen as threatening."

Thomas Moore says: "Obedience means to listen closely to others for words of direction. Only in an ego-mad world do we think that destiny is revealed in our own will and our own thought. You know something that I don't know about where I want to be. If I just listen to myself, I will be trapped in a circle. If you don't speak to me about what you see and what you suspect, then I won't know the direction in which I want to go. And if I don't listen to my friends and neighbors, I'll be stuck in the labyrinth of what I think I want. Obedience is a way of being communal; but if I'm not in community, obedience becomes slavery."

Community means that I give you freedom and I take freedom from you. When it is not in community, then it becomes direction and obedience as a robot and it has nothing to do with life. When we find community, we find obedience, because we have the freedom to share and to take and to give. If we cannot experience freedom in our own lives, then we will never be able to give it to one another. We become the oppressors and others around us become oppressed, and that takes freedom away. It does not give freedom.

When we give one another freedom, we begin to learn how to live as adults. Freedom starts with me. And when it starts with me, then I'm able to give it away because I am not threatened by your freedom, and I'm not threatened by my freedom.

William Arthur Ward: "To laugh is to risk appearing the fool, and to weep is to risk appearing sentimental. To reach for another is to risk involvement, and to expose your feelings is to risk exposing your true self. To place your ideas, your dreams before a crowd, is to risk their loss. To love is to risk not being loved in return. To live is to risk dying. To believe is to risk despair. To try is to risk failure. But risks must be taken because the greatest hazard in life is to risk nothing. The person who risks nothing, who does nothing, who has nothing, is nothing. They may avoid suffering and sorrow, but they cannot learn, feel, change, grow, love or live. Chained by their attitudes, they are slaves and they have forfeited their freedom. Only a person who risks is free. The pessimist complains about the wind; the optimist expects it to change; and the realist adjusts the sails."

Only a person who risks is free. Are you willing to risk? Are you also willing for other people to risk? Can you know freedom? Will you know freedom? Will you give freedom to others that they might be freedom givers again?

2 Corinthians 3:17 says: "Where the Spirit of God is, there is freedom." Let us find our own freedom in action as we give those around us the freedom to be, to grow, change

and become. Then, and only then, will we find the freedom we've always wanted, just the freedom to be.

CHAPTER 9
Dreams 'R' Us

---

8. I WILL BE THE GUARDIAN OF DREAMS NOT OF PRISONS

Knowing our dreams and protecting them are extremely important in this process of taking back our freedom. We must commit to continuously be active in keeping them alive and well. They need to be protected from people and things that would come against them and kill them.

Every day of our lives we have decisions to make about the health and vitality of our dreams. To have a dream or dreams is of utmost importance in our lives as they keep us driving forward to get them accomplished. There are so many outside influences, along with our own insecurities, that want to come against our dreams. Standing firm in our dreams to be all that we can be will take more than just a commitment to stand firm. It actually involves renewing and reevaluating. It means making hard decisions about people and activities in our lives that do not feed the power we need to accomplish our dreams. So, how do we guard our dreams as well as we have guarded our prisons when they seemed so important in our lives? It takes commitment, watchfulness and action.

Seek Out People Who Are Realizing Their Own Dreams

Do you want to be inspired to give yourself permission to realize your dreams in your life? Hang out with someone whose dreams are being accomplished every day of his/her life. There is no better way to learn to keep your dreams alive and well than to spend time with others who are realizing their own dreams. Success does breed success. It comes down to the company we keep. Look around at the people who you spend most of your time with. Are they guardians of their dreams or have they forgotten they ever had a dream. Have they given up on ever being able to accomplish their dreams? Associating with the wrong crowd can bring us down and even let us forget that we have dreams. It can keep us from moving forward to get them accomplished.

The most inspiration you can have is to spend time with others who are being successful in fulfilling their own dreams. Pick up a book about a person who has lived their life in pursuing their dreams. Others are doing it. Others have done it. I know that you, too, want to be in that number. Watch a movie or listen to inspiring stories about those who have or are pursuing successfully their own dreams.

We cannot fly with the eagles when we are stuck on the ground with the turkeys. We can only soar where we are called to fly if we seek out people who are realizing their own dreams and then apply that energy and enthusiasm to accomplish our dreams.

Get Wisdom

Proverbs 4:7, 8 says: "Wisdom is supreme; therefore, get wisdom. Though it cost all you have, get understanding. Esteem her, and she will exalt you; embrace her, and she will honor you."

Wisdom is taking what we know and what we learn and applying it to our journey to realize our dreams. Wisdom is the practical application of what we know intellectually. "Get wisdom"—this phrase shows us the intent and energy that is needed to have wisdom in our lives—we must "get" wisdom—it does not come down from the heavens and fill us up. No, we get wisdom by pursuing it and making it a prime priority in our lives. Wisdom comes not from having more and more knowledge about something. It means taking what we have learned in life and applying it to help us continue on our dream journey.

Ecclesiastes 7:19 packs a lot in this proverb: "Wisdom makes one wise person more powerful than ten rulers in a city."

Wisdom is the key to being a guardian of your dreams and not of your prison. Wisdom will help you to see the importance of getting rid of your prisons and tearing them down. It will show you how to successfully pursue your dreams even in the midst of self-doubt and opposition that will come your way.

Wisdom of Solomon tells us: "Wisdom is more mobile than any other motion; because of her pureness she pervades and penetrates all things. For she is a breath of the power of God, and a pure emanation of the glory of the Almighty; therefore nothing defiled gains entrance into her. For she is the reflection of eternal light, a spotless mirror of the working of God, and an image of God's goodness."

Stay Away From Naysayers

Webster says a naysayer is "one who denies, refuses, opposes, or is skeptical or cynical about something" (or, anything, or everything). Have you ever had a person in your life like that? I'm sure some of us still have people in our lives like that. These are the people, whether they are family, friends or co-workers, who can ruin something beautiful and leave you standing there totally confused about which direction to go next. I have a feeling that many of us spend more time with these people than those that are wise or those who are successfully fulfilling their dreams.

Proverbs 14:7 says: "Stay away from a foolish person, for you will not find knowledge on that person's lips." To be able to stay away from them, we will have to start with identifying who they are. We will then need to decide to move out of the sphere of their influence, especially in regard to our life's dreams.

Naysayers can't and don't want to see anything or anyone succeed. They have decided not to pursue their own dreams and have made it their goal in life to walk around with pins in their hands to burst everyone else's dreams. It is not their intention to take you away from pursuing your dreams, but they end doing just that when you give them the power to ridicule, not support and thwart you from moving forward.

Naysayers can even be the voices in our own heads. They tell us we can never realize our dreams, we need to get back in line and keep the status quo and quit being so determined about our dreams. Our doubts and fears keep us from realizing our dreams and goals. When we couple the naysayers in our heads with those of our family and friends, we end up sitting down and stop moving forward. Stopping the voices of the naysayers can be the most important step to pursuing and realizing our dreams. We are so afraid of being different, launching out on our own and trusting God that we sit in our pool of self-pity and let the negative voices drown out what we want to do and who we want to be.

Practice The Gift Of Giving
And The Gift Of Receiving

Matthew 10:8 states: "Freely you have received, freely give." You might ask what giving and receiving have to do with being a guardian of my dreams instead of my prisons.

Giving is one of the greatest virtues that we can live. Likewise, receiving is just as important. It is a circle that is unending. Many people want to know why they never receive anything. My first guess is that they are not giving wholeheartedly and have broken the unending circle. We all have excuses as to why "I can't give," whether it is to another person, a great cause or the world in general, but those excuses will never allow us to move forward with our dreams.

Making a commitment to being a giver and a receiver means that we can teach others the gift of giving and receiving. When we demonstrate and teach those principles, we, then, reap the benefits of their generous giving along with their ability to receive from us and others.

As we pursue our dreams, we will learn that giving is one of the keys to moving forward. But, you say, "I don't have anything to give." You may not if you have given up on your dreams and bowed down to the naysayers. However, when we are wholeheartedly committed to pursuing our dreams and the world conspires with us to accomplish them, we will have an abundance of ideas, encouragement, money, time and wisdom to share with those around us. We are no longer limited by fear about giving because we have learned to be generous to ourselves and the world by pursuing our dreams. Our dream journey demands the spirit of giving and receiving. It is how we move forward and gather the wisdom and support that we need along the way.

We receive help, encouragement and strength and we turn around and give it back. It takes many forms, but the principle is still the same: give to get, get to give.

God, the universe, karma—whatever you want to call it—is the principle of "what goes around comes around" or "you reap what you sow." The principle of giving and receiving are so important on our dream journeys. It brings wisdom and people who can encourage you on your journey. It brings resources you never knew that might be available. You can, then, turn around and give that away as you have received it and the whole process takes place again.

Our generosity in giving and receiving are key elements to being guardians of our dreams. Those who want to remain in isolation in their prisons can be a world unto themselves. If you truly want to pursue your dreams and accomplish them, you must cultivate a spirit of generosity in your life. This opens your world to share with others who, in turn, will share with you.

Our dreams must find their fruition in our world. It is for this very reason that you are alive and here in this place and time. Don't let the world miss out on your dreams and your life. Make a difference. Dream your dreams. Live your dreams. Encourage others in their dreams. Make a difference right where you are every moment of every day.

Hang with those who know what their dreams are and are pursuing them. Get wisdom and stay away from naysayers. Take all the world has to give you and then give back. Those are the keys and practices of being the guardian of your dreams and not of your prisons.

CHAPTER 10
What The World Needs Now

---

9. I WILL REMEMBER THAT MY DREAMS ARE IMPORTANT TO THE WORLD

Remembering that our dreams are important to our world is not always easy. We have forgotten that we have something to give that the world needs. We become busy with our lives and forget that we have something special and unique to share with the world. Our dreams get put on a shelf or we become discouraged and don't pursue our dreams and goals in life.

The importance of accomplishing our dreams in life means that we have to remember that they are something that no one else can accomplish in the same manner that we can. Forgetting is very easy because it takes energy to keep our dreams moving forward. Dreaming is one thing. Doing is another.

Remembering Our Dreamers

When we can bring to mind dreamers that have made a difference in their world, hopefully we can be inspired to move forward in being our unique self with what we have to offer the world. We remember their determination, their passion and their ability to change the world in which they live(d).

Who is on your list of dreamers who got it done: Martin Luther King, Jr., Mother Theresa, Jesus, one of our presidents, a teacher, a family member, a friend, a celebrity, a sports person, a leader? Moses was a great dreamer and saw the Promised Land in his vision. It's what kept him on track in moving the people of Israel through the wilderness after they left Egypt. Most of the time it wasn't easy, but he kept his eyes on the bigger picture and then moved forward to get it accomplished.

Remembering our dreamers inspires us and reenergizes us. These people were just ordinary people with a unique dream they were willing to live for or to die for. They did whatever it took to get their mission accomplished. No matter what the opposition, they knew what their dream was and drove around the opposition to get it done. Our dreamers are the heroes of our lives and our world. They know where they are going and they are/were willing to pay the price for getting it done.

We can only accomplish the purpose of our lives by remembering others who have gone before us and who have been courageous enough to make a change in the world in which they lived.

It's All About Me

You must say to yourself: "No one else has my dream. No one else can get it accomplished with the tools and resources that I have. No one can take my dream away from me unless I let them. No one else is me. I am unique. I am special. I have dreams that no one else has. I have ways to get it done that no one else has. Being all that I'm called to be and accomplishing my part in changing the world cannot be done by anyone else but me."

It is all about me. Not in a self-centered way ("the world revolves around me"), but in the uniqueness of my life and experiences and calling. Each one of us is important in this world. We forget how uniquely each of us is created and that that creation is here for a purpose. Instead, we tend to "go with the flow" and let other people persuade us not to go against the tide. We allow them to distract us from what we, uniquely, can accomplish in this world.

All of us are terminal. No one gets out of this alive. All the dreamers of the world were also terminal. Yet, they still moved forward every day to make their dreams change the world. When we get out of our prisons of low self-worth, fear, doubt, insecurity, fear of risking and fearing what others will think, we can stand up and say "my life is all about this dream or direction or act of servanthood."

Some of us don't want it to be all about me. We want others to tell us what to do, how to act and what we should and should not pursue. Getting out of our prisons and moving forward in making our lives worthwhile means that we will definitely encounter opposition and maybe even ridicule. It comes back, however, to taking responsibility for my life and my dreams and for making them a part of the change of the world in the generation in which I live.

Dreams Must Have Feet

Dreams are wonderful things in our lives that can remain dreams all of our lives. However, they must take action and grow feet and move forward toward being accomplished in our lives. Having dreams is important, but, more importantly, realizing our dreams and doing what it takes to make them happen is most important.

James Dean said: "Dream as if you will live forever, live as if you'll die today." Harriet Tubman (Abolitionist and American escaped slave) said: "Every great dream begins with a dreamer. Always remember, you have within you the strength, the patience, and the passion to reach for the stars to change the world." It is all about you and your willingness to go beyond the ordinary and make a difference. You are not like anybody else before you or after you. This is your moment. This is your life. These are your dreams. Live them and never let go of them.

Dreams Can Change The World

When we remember the dreamers in our world, not only in our past, but also in our present, we see that the world can change. Sometimes it is a very small section of people who are changed or a very small problem is addressed and solved, but it is the gift and energy needed for just that specific time and place. Dreams can change the world—but they have to get out of our heads, onto paper or our computer and grow feet. Our dreams must move from where they are doing nothing to a place where all is being accomplished and they are moving forward.

We are the energy. We are the force. We can no longer be victims or prisoners. We must have no prisons to return to and no "safe places" that will keep us from forging ahead.

William Hutchinson Murray (one of the founders of Rhode Island) said it so eloquently: "Until one is committed, there is hesitancy, the chance to draw back, always ineffectiveness. Concerning all acts of initiative and creation, there is one elementary truth the ignorance of which kills countless ideas and splendid plans: that the moment one definitely commits oneself, the providence moves too. A whole stream of events issues from the decision, raising in one's favor all manner of unforeseen incidents, meetings and material assistance, which no person could have dreamt would have come their way."

In the religious and spiritual circles, that is called faith. It is not tangible. It is not something that can be put into a written plan or onto a spread sheet. It is the necessity of letting go and letting God. Our lives become limited by what we can't or won't do. Our lives become unlimited when we step out of that comfort zone and trust that we will see open and closed doors as we move forward. It is all about you. It is up to you. You can live today in fulfilling your part of the greater work here on earth, or you can merely take up space and let others direct your life while you watch them fulfilling their own dreams.

When I remember it is all about me, then I can give myself permission to dream and live my dreams. Holding back in fear and inactivity will only result in my part of the world dream being thwarted.

I will remember that my dreams are important to the world. Fear can stop us at any point in time. Finances or lack of finances can keep us from moving forward if we let them immobilize our movement forward and commitment to change this world one life at a time.

"What the World Needs Now" is your dreams and your actions to fulfill those dreams. Become empowered in your dreams and your life. Make a difference. Share your dreams. Live your dreams.

I WILL REMEMBER THAT MY DREAMS ARE IMPORTANT TO THE WORLD

CHAPTER 11
Living And Giving Freedom

---

10. I WILL ENCOURAGE FREEDOM OF THOUGHT, FREEDOM OF EXPRESSION AND FREEDOM TO BE

As Americans, we want our freedoms. We demand them, celebrate them, fight for them and revel in them. But, somehow, when it comes to our personal freedom to be who we are and allowing others their personal freedom to be who they are, we aren't so good at "being all that we can be."

John 8:32 says: "You will know the truth and the truth will set you free." If we are not teaching and living a truth that sets people free to be who they are and to realize their dreams in life, we are living a lie that is not the truth that we have been given to share.

When we understand what freedom is all about, it makes no difference where we are, in what country we live, or whether we're in jail, or whether we're free. We have freedom because we choose to have freedom. Freedom is ours for the taking. It is always available if we want to have it. It can be abused. It can be a gift. It can be taken for granted or it can be truly experienced.

When we give ourselves freedom, we begin to learn how to live as adults. The hardest thing about having my freedom is that then I have to give you freedom.

Freedom of Thought

This is the freedom to think, dream and plan. It is the freedom to never have a doubt about who I am and to know that whatever may come into my life, I know who I am. Our dreams will never be realized unless it first begins in our minds and our thoughts and our plans. We have two enemies when it comes to really having freedom of thought in our lives: ourselves and others. It seems that sabotage is the greatest enemy to the freedom of thought.

When we begin thinking that we have the freedom to dream and to realize our dreams, our inner voices and the outer voices of others come against us. They make us doubt, have fear and convince us that we can never really live our dreams.

The greatest problem with the church and our society today is that it has needed and wanted to control. As we study Jesus' ministry, we never see that He had to control anyone. He displayed the fact that He knew that God was in complete control and that his job was to listen and obey what it was that God wanted him to do. The church through the centuries has taken over people's lives in many areas that it has never been asked to do. The people, however, have also allowed this to happen.

Freedom of Expression

Being able to express our dreams, our successes, our failures and our hopes for the future is the strongest component on the road to seeing the realization of our dreams. We must be able to bounce ideas off others and explain what it is that we are seeing in our dreams.

When we talk about our dreams and share them with others, we are truly risking their acceptance or rejection. Many of us stop at the point of never sharing. When we do risk and share our dreams, we are completely crushed when no one can support us. We are devastated when someone outright demolishes our dreams through their own reactions or lack thereof. Proverbs tells us that there is power in the tongue—the power of life and death. The freedom of expression means that we are speaking our dreams and giving them life.

Psalm 119:45: "I will walk about in freedom, for I have sought out your precepts." How often we wear our

116

shame—our shame of who we are or what our dreams are. We wear the shame that we take upon ourselves that refuses to give us freedom. We don't stand proud! We don't walk around like we're God's children. We walk and talk like we are ashamed, like we are carrying and wearing our shame. We need to walk and talk in freedom, David says in this Psalm. We need to walk and talk in freedom because we know who God is, and God knows who we are.

Freedom To Be

This is the freedom just to be who we really are, realizing our dreams, expressing our dreams and making them happen. To be a dreamer is risky business, but when we realize that God has given dreams to each of us because of who we uniquely are, then we will begin to revel in those dreams and the dreams will become who we truly are. They will not be separate from who I am, they will be me. They will be the very essence of my being and my personality and my life. They will not be me and them. They will be me and me.

Our dreams are not about "pie in the sky." They are about the here and now, the essence of who we are and will be. They are not something that can be left in the dreaming state and never fulfilled.

The freedom to be is a glorious, dangerous place to find ourselves. It knows no boundaries or limits. It cannot be held back or dumbed down. It cannot be suppressed or chained. The freedom to be means that we stop being slaves to ourselves and to others. Being a slave limits us again to the prisons that we have vowed to tear down and destroy. And, hopefully, we have also committed not to build any new prisons back on the old foundations. The freedom to be takes us from mediocrity and a ho-hum life to a fulfillment that only comes when we are who we are supposed to be and we are doing what we have been called to do.

Stepping out of the norm and heading for the clouds has never been easy, but it is the call to freedom that we follow, not the call to imprisonment and a lackluster life.

Those whom we fear have great power over us. Our greatest enemy is not some outside opponent. It is the fear within us. "Am I doing it right?" "What if I fail?" "What if I don't understand it correctly?" "What if I'm not in the same place on the journey of life that somebody else is?" "What if I just can't do it?" "What if?" "What if?" "What if?" The fear is so great that we make no movement forward to make our dreams come true and give ourselves just the freedom to be. When we no longer dream and act on our dreams, we become frozen. We become ineffective in realizing our own freedom to be. We become deterrents to others because we can't show others what it means to have the freedom to be.

Freedom For Me And You

Freedom is free...but we have made it something to be earned, learned or found by the lucky few. The freedom that is free is free. It is not encumbered by rules and regulations. It does not look the same for everybody. It is freedom and that breeds more freedom.

Freedom is a journey, not a destination. It is a journey in growth and moving forward. There is so much bondage everywhere. People need the keys to unlock the door and get out. We need to get freedom where we can be ourselves and allow others to be who they are called to be.

It is the freedom to be, which becomes the power to be, which becomes the freedom to be, which becomes the power to be. The circle never ends.

God delights in our very good creation. God delights when we have freedom and when we give freedom.

Tear down the walls of your prisons, walk out into the light where you can see again the freedom to dream. Recapture who you are and who God has created you to be. Live in freedom. Give in freedom. Make today, and every day you live, the first day of the rest of your life—free, courageous, generous, strong and authentic.

CHAPTER 12
Moving On

EMANCIPATION PROCLAMATION

We come to the beginning of our Emancipation Proclamation. Noting that this is the last chapter, you were probably expecting me to say, "This is the end." Hopefully this will be the beginning where you apply all the information we have learned together. There are so many practical steps in this book on moving forward to realize our dreams. Some of us are having a hard time identifying our dreams because we have suppressed them so long that we no longer remember what they are.

Part of the process of getting out of our prisons is getting out of the prison of forgetfulness in regard to our dreams. Some of us have given up on our dreams because of fear, ridicule, laziness, lack of initiative, lack of support and a myriad of other reasons. These prisons have held us captive and have caused us to abandon dreams that can only be pursued in freedom. We will have to move out of the prison of forgetfulness and hurt and move to recapture those dreams and make them happen.

Philippians 4:12, 13: "I know what it is to be in need, and I know what it is to have plenty." (Paul says he knows what it is like to live in prisons—prisons of need and prisons of plenty.) "I have learned the secret of being content in any and every situation, whether well fed or hungry, whether living in plenty or in want. I can do everything through the one who gives me strength."

Here is the essence of moving out of our prisons and moving into freedom to accomplish our life's dreams and goals. It is finding the secret and living it every moment of our lives.

No More Whining

Nobody wants to hear it. We whine about everything in our lives. The greatest reason we whine about things in our lives is that it keeps us from actually doing anything about it. We whine about the weather, our jobs, our spouses, our money (or lack thereof), our politicians, the unfairness of life, our lack of friends or influence, those in power and those different from us.

Our whining knows no boundaries and no limits. We think everyone really cares about our whining when, in reality, we whine to hear ourselves talk. It gets us nowhere. It resolves nothing. It does not lead to fulfilling our dreams and goals. It makes us less attractive to those around us and causes us to live and dwell in negativity which can also lead to living in isolation. We move to the place where we feel like whining is our goal and dream in life. We fall into a pattern of looking for things to whine about as that is what our life is about.

No More Procrastinating

To realize our dreams and live our Emancipation Proclamation, we will have to cease procrastinating in our lives and move forward to get things done.

It will take a decision and determination. It will take a plan and action. It will take getting up off our "buts" and butts. We must stop making excuses for why our lives are not being what we want them to be. Procrastination ceases when you do something...not just wishful thinking and hoping that things might just get better on their own.

Procrastination is linked to fear, laziness, immobility, excuses, poor time-management and lack of focus and direction. To fully realize our personhood and our dreams, we must stop procrastinating. There is no day like today to get started and to accomplish something (even something very small) toward your emancipation and freedom.

No More Blaming

How we like to blame everyone for the mess we're in! We blame them for the prisons we are in and the lack of movement forward in our lives. It's our parents' fault, society's fault, the government's fault, our boss's fault, the system's fault, our education's fault, our lack or excess of money, someone else's decisions, circumstances, luck, fate. We want it to be everyone else's fault but mine. If I ultimately take responsibility for where I am in life, I can take ultimate responsibility for where I want to be and where I want to go.

Blaming others or other things for our lack of moving forward or getting our life on track only leads to more failure and not getting it done. Our lives cannot be built upon the lack of responsibility on our own parts or on the blame that we want to place outside ourselves. My dreams and my life are my responsibility. I make it or break it, no matter what comes into my path. This does not mean that it will all be smooth sailing. It does mean that I will be responsible for my life, my dreams, my freedom and my movement forward.

No More Victims

To fully realize who we are and to realize our dreams in life, we must stop being the victim. Being the victim allows us to move to a point of hurt and resignation instead of growing, learning and becoming. Being a victim means that I not only blame someone or something else, but I choose to live my life in a subordinate position to that person or thing. I actually give away all my power to move forward and I live my life in the shadow of that person or thing.

A victim always has the "poor me" mentality and lives as if they have no control or ability to do what they want to do because this other thing is always bigger than they are. It is so easy to play the victim because it always lets this "other" run our lives. We simply just cannot do anything about it. We have to choose to be a victim. It is our choice.

We can also choose to stop being the victim. It may take professional help, a support group, a decision, therapy, etc. We can truly stop being the victim and learn to find freedom from that mode of living.

No More Excuses

Making excuses is one of the easiest ways of avoiding being emancipated from the prisons that can control our lives. We want to make an excuse as to why we're stuck. We truly believe that everyone will understand why it is that we are here at this point in our lives. Making excuses is just a rationalization to ourselves as to why we're not moving forward. We look for a list of reasons why we can't be free to be ourselves. We invent a list so we can review it ourselves and offer it to others for their sympathy and empathy. We, then, feel justified in losing out on the dreams that we pretend we want so badly.

There are lots of excuses out there (true or false) as to why we are not finding our freedom or being all we are called to be. But, they will never contribute to our true freedom. We must be willing to put aside excuses (which really are only lies) and take our own responsibility to be who we are called to be. We will, then, be able to leave them behind and move ahead.

No More Not Trusting God

We don't trust God. Paul says in our Philippians passage: "I can do everything through the one who gives me strength (empowers me)." It doesn't just come from ourselves. God, the universe, the spirit of love, whatever you call it, conspires with us to succeed when we make a determination and movement forward to where we want to go and who we want to be. The word everything means exactly that: everything. There is nothing in our lives that we cannot do or cannot overcome with our Higher Power's help. Our greatest problem is not God. Our greatest problem is our inability to trust that God can and will be there when we take the initiative and move out.

The world is waiting for our dreams to come to fruition. There is no one in the world that has your dream(s) or your unique ability to accomplish them. You don't have to change the world, you may only have to change the world you touch every day. But, no one else can live your dreams or change your world but you. Step out of your fears and hesitancy and step into a world of freedom and excitement. Run out of your prisons, do the work to tear them down and destroy the foundations and move on to build your dreams and be all you have been called to be. You can do it. Only you can do it your way.

Demolish your prisons.

Step out of the darkness.

Give wings to your dreams.

Breathe the fresh air of freedom.

Just "BE!"